MEXICO
the land

Bobbie Kalman

The Lands, Peoples, and Cultures Series

Crabtree Publishing Company

The Lands, Peoples, and Cultures Series
Created by Bobbie Kalman

For Fruzan and Ian

Editor-in-Chief
Bobbie Kalman

Writing team
Bobbie Kalman
David Schimpky

Editors
Tammy Everts
David Schimpky
Janine Schaub
Lynda Hale
Petrina Gentile

Illustrations
Antoinette "Cookie" DeBiasi

Design and computer layout
Lynda Hale
Antoinette "Cookie" DeBiasi

Printer
Worzalla Publishing Company

Separations and film
Book Art Inc.

Special thanks to: Jürgen Bavoni, Canadian International Development Agency, Monique Denis, Irene Herrera, Library of Congress, Laurie Taylor, and Pierre Vachon

Photographs
Jürgen Bavoni: pages 8 (bottom), 11 (top), 20 (bottom)
Jim Bryant: cover, pages 3, 4-5, 6, 9 (both), 11 (middle), 12 (bottom), 13 (bottom left, bottom right), 20 (top), 22 (bottom), 23, 26 (top left), 26-27
CIDA/David Barbour: pages 14, 24 (inset), 26 (circle)
Peter Crabtree and Bobbie Kalman: title page, pages 8 (top), 12-13, 16-17, 21
James Kamstra: pages 11 (bottom), 16 (left), 21 (inset), 22 (top, middle), 28, 29 (all), 30 (both)
Diane Payton Majumdar: pages 7, 15, 24, 25
Superstock/Steve Vidler: pages 18-19

Published by
Crabtree Publishing Company

350 Fifth Avenue	360 York Road, RR 4,	73 Lime Walk
Suite 3308	Niagara-on-the-Lake,	Headington
New York	Ontario, Canada	Oxford OX3 7AD
N.Y. 10118	L0S 1J0	United Kingdom

Cataloguing in Publication Data
Kalman, Bobbie, 1947-
    Mexico: the land

(The Lands, Peoples, and Cultures Series)
Includes index.
ISBN 0-86505-214-X (library bound) ISBN 0-86505-294-8 (pbk.)
This book looks at the land of Mexico, including its history, regions, natural resources, wildlife, environmental problems, and transportation systems.

1. Mexico - Description and travel - Juvenile literature.
I. Title. II. Series.

F1216.5.K35 1993   j972

Contents

4   The land of Mexico

6   The struggle for a nation

10   Regions of Mexico

14   Earthquake!

16   Volcanoes

18   Resources, business, and industry

23   Agriculture

25   Transportation

26   Mexico's cities

28   Wildlife and the environment

31   Glossary

32   Index

The land of Mexico

There is a legend about Hernán Cortés, the Spanish adventurer who conquered the Aztec civilization in Mexico. In 1528 he was called back to Spain to report on the New World. The king, curious about his new empire, asked him to describe the land of Mexico. Cortés picked up a piece of paper, crumpled it, and tossed it on a table. "This is Mexico," he said.

The gesture illustrated how mountainous the land of Mexico was, but Cortés failed to show the beauty and variety of the land with his demonstration. Mexico is dry deserts and lush rainforests; it is rolling hills and broad plains. Modern Mexico is also full of contrasts: there are factories and farms, huge cities and small towns, populated areas and untouched wilderness.

✺ The struggle for a nation ✺

People were living in North America long before Europeans "discovered" the continent. It is believed that, as many as 40,000 years ago, Asians crossed a sand bar or an ice bridge in the Bering Strait to Alaska. By 20,000 BC, some of these people had migrated as far south as Mexico. Several of these groups developed into advanced **civilizations**. A civilization is a society that achieves a great deal in arts and sciences.

The Olmecs
The Olmecs were the first major civilization in Mexico. They began building monuments in the thick forests of the eastern coast around 1200 BC. Archaeologists have uncovered a site, called San Lorenzo, that is believed to have been used by the Olmecs for religious ceremonies. The most striking features of San Lorenzo are huge heads that are carved from rock. Some of these heads are over three meters (nine feet) tall!

The Classic period
People who study ancient Mexican civilizations refer to the years between AD 100 and 900 as the Classic period. Native cultures were at their height during this time. Cities, consisting of huge pyramids, temples, and homes, were built across Mexico. The Native civilizations gained much knowledge of the natural world. They also recorded their history and beliefs accurately. During the Classic period, southern Mexico was dotted with cities built by the Zapotecs. The metropolis of Teotihuacán dominated central Mexico. The most famous civilization of the Classic period is the Mayan. Mayan cities were built across the Yucatán Peninsula and Central America. The Mayan civilization and the city of Teotihuacán declined by AD 900. The reason is still a mystery. Today, all that remains of the great cities are archaeological sites and ruins that are still covered by thick rainforest.

The Aztecs

The Aztec empire was the last great Native civilization in Mexico. The Aztecs were originally **nomadic**, which means they moved from place to place. Eventually, they settled in central Mexico. They were great warriors who conquered neighboring tribes and established a vast empire. The center of the Aztec empire was a large city called Tenochtitlán, which was built on an island in Lake Texcoco. Although modern-day Mexico City is built over the Aztec capital, several temples and pyramids are still standing.

Spanish conquest

The culture of Mexico's Native civilizations changed in 1519 when Hernán Cortés landed on the Gulf coast of Mexico. The Spanish adventurer had heard stories of a kingdom of riches and came with 400 soldiers. The Aztecs were hated by other Native groups, and Cortés found plenty of allies to help fight them. By 1521 the Aztec ruler Montezuma II had been killed, and Spain had taken control of Mexico. The country was named New Spain. It was part of the large Spanish empire in North and South America.

Montezuma and the Spaniards

Quetzalcoatl was considered the most powerful of the Aztec gods. The Aztecs believed he had gone away but would one day return. At the time that Quetzalcoatl's return was expected, the Aztecs heard rumors of strange creatures approaching from the north. The Aztecs wondered if these strangers might be Quetzalcoatl and his followers.

When he saw the pale-faced men, the Aztec leader Montezuma II fell to his knees before the one he thought was Quetzalcoatl. Montezuma offered him the city of Tenochtitlán.

Too late, the Aztecs learned that Quetzalcoatl and his followers were actually the explorer Hernán Cortés and his army. Though the Aztecs fought to regain their city, they were unsuccessful. The Aztecs were defeated, and Tenochtitlán was lost.

(opposite page) **The city of Palenque contains some of the best-preserved Mayan buildings in Mexico.**
(below) **This stone carving shows the meeting of Montezuma II and Hernán Cortés.**

Colony and independence

For nearly 300 years the Spanish controlled Mexico. During this period, many Spanish and Native Mexicans married and had children. Their descendants are called *mestizos* and, today, they are the largest ethnic group in Mexico.

The Spanish rulers gained great wealth by taxing the people and forcing them to mine silver and gold. In 1810, however, the Mexican people rose up against their rulers. The leader of this revolution was a priest named Father Hidalgo. Although he was captured and executed in 1811, he is considered the father of modern Mexico. In 1821 the revolution ended, and Mexico was finally free from Spanish rule.

Years of turmoil

The next few decades were filled with war and turmoil. In 1836 the Mexican province of Texas declared independence. In a war with the United States, which lasted from 1846 to 1848, other northern territories were lost as well. In 1863 the French army invaded Mexico and made a European archduke named Maximilian emperor. His rule lasted a brief four years. When the French troops withdrew, Maximilian was captured and executed.

Foreigners owned the land

The years between 1867 and 1910 were free from war. During much of this time, Mexico was ruled by a dictator named Porfirio Díaz. He allowed wealthy Mexicans and foreign companies to control Mexico's economy. Huge ranches, sometimes up to 6 million hectares (15 million acres) in size, were run by rich land barons. Foreign investors controlled the mining industry. During this time, the Mexican peasants were overworked, underpaid, and forced to live in terrible conditions. They had no opportunity to improve their lives because all the good land was owned by the wealthy. These poor living standards led to the revolution of 1910, in which peasants fought to gain land. The long and bloody war ended in 1920 and, since then, Mexico has had a peaceful and stable government.

Modern government

There are two levels of government in Mexico. The central government is located in the capital, Mexico City. The head of the country is the president, who is elected every six years. The congress creates and passes laws. There are many political parties in Mexico, but the most powerful is the Institutional Revolutionary Party. It has controlled the government for most of the last 60 years.

The second level of government is that of the states. Mexico is a federation of 31 states and one federal district. Each is administered by an elected governor.

The people of Mexico

Mexicans come from a variety of backgrounds. Most are *mestizos*. Native Mexicans are descendants of the people who lived in Mexico long before Cortés arrived. Other groups include **mulattos**, who are of mixed Native and African heritage, and *criollos*, who are of European or American backgrounds.

Rising population

Mexico has a high population, and its numbers are growing. As a result, Mexico is becoming a nation of young people—one-third of the population is under the age of fifteen! The high population is a special challenge for Mexico, as the government tries to provide jobs and services for everyone.

(top) Beautiful cities, filled with majestic churches and fine houses, were built when Mexico was a Spanish colony. They are called "colonial cities."
(bottom) Red, green, and white are the colors of Mexico's flag. Flags are a common sight on patriotic holidays.
(opposite page, top) The young people of Mexico are full of hope for their future.
(opposite page, bottom) The Angel of Independence is located on a wide street called the Paseo de la Reforma in Mexico City. It reminds Mexicans of their difficult fight for freedom.

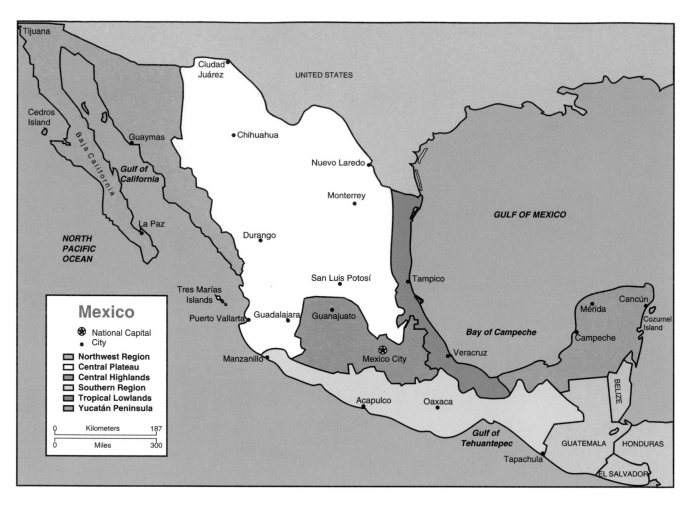

🦎 Regions of Mexico 🦎

Although Mexico is divided into states, it is easier to think of the country in terms of its regions. Each region has features that make it unique. For example, the volcanoes of the Central Highlands are very different from the hills of Chiapas or the deserts of Baja California.

The Central Highlands

The most heavily populated region in Mexico is the Central Highlands. This area sits on a high plateau, surrounded on three sides by mountains. To the east is the Sierra Madre Oriental. To the west is the Sierra Madre Occidental, and to the south is the Neo-volcanic Cordillera. It is in this last range that you can find most of Mexico's volcanoes, including Orizaba—Mexico's tallest mountain. In the Aztec language, it is called Citlaltépetl, which means "star mountain." The Central Highlands are also home to the majority of Mexico's lakes. Lakes Chapala and Pátzcuaro are among the largest lakes in Mexico.

Northwest deserts

Northwest Mexico, made up of Baja California and the states of Sonora and Sinaloa, is the most isolated part of the country. The land is dry, hot, and barren. Some deserts in this area have hardy vegetation, but others, such as the Algodones Dunes, support little life. There is some vegetation around the Gulf of California, as well as a few fertile spots, called **oases,** which are fed by underground springs.

The Central Plateau

Two long mountain ranges follow the Pacific and Gulf coasts of Mexico. To the west is the steep Sierra Madre Occidental, and to the east is the rolling Sierra Madre Oriental. Between these two ranges lies the Central Plateau. This high-altitude area is dry, though not as hot and dry as the northwest. It has few rivers or lakes. Mining, ranching, farming, and forestry are among the industries operating in this region.

(above) The Barranca del Cobre (the Copper Canyon) is located in the state of Chihuahua. This landform is even deeper than the Grand Canyon in Arizona.
(middle) The Central Plateau stretches as far as the eye can see!
(bottom) The cholla cactus is one of the few plants that lives in Mexico's deserts.

The tropical lowlands

The Gulf Lowlands follow the eastern coast of Mexico from Tamaulipas state to the state of Veracruz. This flat plain lies between the Gulf of Mexico and the Sierra Madre Oriental mountain range. Its tropical climate makes it an ideal home for many different kinds of plants and animals.

The mountainous south

In the Southern Region, winters are warm and dry, whereas summers are hot and humid. Several mountain ranges, including the Sierra Madre del Sur, the Sierra Madre de Oaxaca, and the Sierra de Soconusco are located in this region. Dry, deciduous forests still stand in some northern parts of this sparsely populated region. Thick rainforest makes up the vegetation in the southern Chiapas state. Unfortunately, heavy logging has destroyed many of the forested areas in the south.

The Yucatán Peninsula

The most eastern part of Mexico is the Yucatán Peninsula, which juts into the Gulf of Mexico. The Yucatán is a flat, low-lying limestone shelf covered by tropical forest. Limestone dissolves easily, so the peninsula is full of caverns and underground rivers. A feature unique to this area is the **sinkhole**. A sinkhole forms when the ground between a cavern and the earth's surface grows too thin and collapses. Sinkholes can cause damage to buildings and roads.

(top) Mexico's Pacific coast is a favorite destination for tourists.
(bottom) Thick rainforest covers much of southern Mexico.
(opposite page, bottom left) Deep in the wilderness of Chiapas lies the Cascada Agua Azul, which means "cascade of azure water."
(opposite page, bottom right) Central Mexico's many hills make house-building a challenging task!

✒ Earthquake! ✒

Earthquakes are one of the world's most deadly natural disasters. The ground shakes, causing buildings to collapse. Huge cracks can open up on the earth's surface. Water pipes and power lines are torn, leaving thousands of people without water or electricity. Gas lines are broken. The leaking gas causes fires and explosions. Mexico has been shaken by earthquakes several times. One of the worst earthquakes hit Mexico City in 1985, killing about 9000 people.

Shifting plates

Why have so many earthquakes occurred in one country? The answer may lie in a theory called **plate tectonics**. The earth is composed of several layers. The **core** is the center of the earth.

The thick layer surrounding the core is called the **mantle**. The **crust** is a thin layer that makes up the surface of the earth. Scientists believe that the crust is made up of several different **plates**, which are constantly moving. Some move away from other plates, some move toward other plates, and some rub sideways against one another. At the spots where the plates touch, the ground often shakes with vibrations called **tremors**. Severe tremors are called earthquakes.

Mexico is located at a point where four plates meet. These are the North American plate, the Pacific plate, the Caribbean plate, and the Cocos plate. The shifting of these plates causes the many earthquakes in Mexico.

Protection from earthquakes

Thousands of people died in the 1985 earthquake in Mexico City because buildings collapsed. The tremors shook the buildings so violently that they fell— big and small buildings alike. Engineers are now designing sturdy buildings that will not collapse during an earthquake.

Scientists, called **seismologists**, who study earthquakes are also working to find ways of predicting when and where an earthquake will strike. With proper warning, people will be able to take safety precautions.

(opposite page) Thousands of homes in and around Mexico City were destroyed during the 1985 earthquake.
(right) Mexico City's tallest building, the Latin American Tower, survived the 1985 earthquake because it is built on hundreds of posts driven deep into the ground.
(below) This diagram shows where the plates of the earth's crust meet in Mexico.

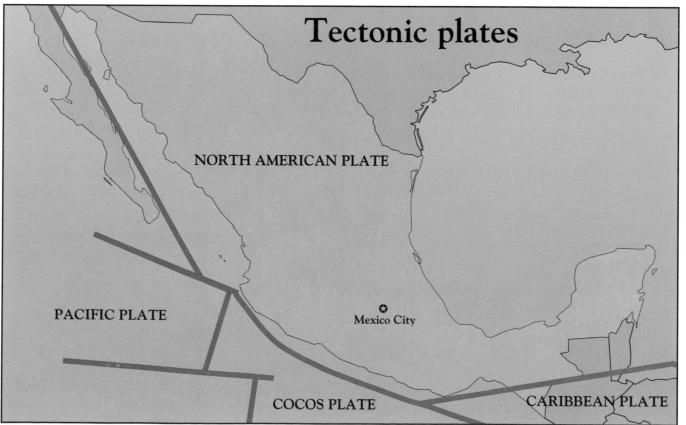

Tectonic plates

NORTH AMERICAN PLATE

PACIFIC PLATE

⊛
Mexico City

COCOS PLATE

CARIBBEAN PLATE

🦎 Volcanoes 🦎

There are three types of volcanoes. Volcanoes that no longer erupt are called **extinct**. A volcano that has not erupted for a long time, but may still become active, is called **dormant**. If lava, ash, or smoke is coming out of a volcano, that volcano is called **active**. Mexico is home to several volcanoes, most of which are located in an area west of Mexico City. Some have names, such as Citlaltépetl and Popocatépetl, that date from Aztec times.

How volcanoes work

Like earthquakes, volcanoes are found in areas where the plates of the earth's crust meet. Big chunks of the crust are forced down into the high temperatures of the mantle. The crust melts, forming liquid rock called **magma**. The magma rises through cracks in the earth's crust. When it reaches the surface, it is called **lava**. The lava cools and becomes rock. Eventually, the layers of lava build up and form a high **cone**. The formation of a cone can occur quickly. In 1943 a Mexican volcano called Paricutín grew 137 meters (450 feet) in one week! It eventually reached a height of 518 meters (1700 feet).

Eruption!

Sometimes volcanoes erupt. Although volcanic eruptions can happen very slowly, many are violent and can destroy surrounding areas. A violent eruption occurs when the top of a volcano is sealed with cooled lava. The pressure within the volcano builds until the volcano suddenly bursts, expelling gas, steam, ash, rock fragments, and rivers of lava. Fortunately, scientists are learning more about volcanoes. They hope to be able to predict when a volcano will erupt, so people who live nearby can seek safety.

(above) The flow of lava from a volcano creates a landscape that looks like the surface of the moon! (opposite page, top) Though it is still active, the summit of Popocatépetl is covered year-round by snow. (opposite page, bottom) This diagram shows what occurs inside an erupting volcano.

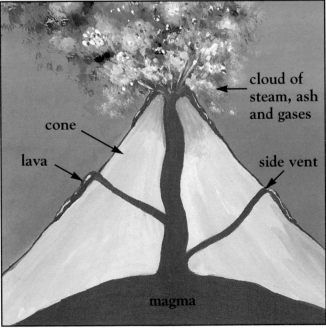

cloud of
steam, ash
and gases

cone

lava

side vent

magma

Volcano of the warrior

There is an Aztec legend about the volcano called
Popocatépetl (shown above) and a nearby
mountain called Iztaccíhuatl. There was once a
mighty warrior and a princess who were in love.
One day there was a great battle in which the
warrior was victorious. Unfortunately, his enemies
sent word to the princess that the warrior was
dead, and she died of a broken heart. When the
warrior returned and heard the news, he was very
sad. In his grief, he built two great mountains. He
placed the princess's body on the mountain called
Iztaccíhuatl, which means "sleeping woman."
He then stood on the volcano of Popocatépetl,
which means "smoking mountain," holding a
torch lit in her memory.

Resources, business, and industry

Mexico is rich in **natural resources**. Natural resources include such things as oil, minerals, forests, fish, and water. Some of these resources are used by the Mexican people; some are sold to other countries. Besides natural resources, Mexico has many other advantages. The beauty of its landscapes and its good weather have contributed to its huge tourism industry. Many factories have been built in Mexico to benefit from low wages and energy costs. Despite these advantages, Mexico still has high unemployment. There are simply too many people and not enough jobs.

Hydroelectric power

Many of Mexico's rivers have been dammed and used for hydroelectric projects. **Hydroelectricity** uses fast water to drive turbines, which in turn create electrical power. There are large hydroelectric projects on the Río Tonto, the Río Balsas, and the Río Grijalva (*río* means "river"). The damming of rivers has met with opposition from some of Mexico's Native groups. A hydroelectric project on the Río Balsas threatens many Native villages. The project will flood their villages and farmland and destroy their ancient monuments.

Oil

Crude oil, or **petroleum**, is what oil is called before it is refined. After the refining process, oil is ready to be used. Oil is very important to Mexico's economy. The first oil wells were developed in 1901. By the end of World War I, Mexico was one of the world's greatest oil-producing nations. Today, all of Mexico's oil fields are managed by **Pemex**, which stands for Petróleos Mexicanos. Pemex controls all aspects of Mexico's petroleum industry, including exploration, drilling, and export. In the late 1970s, oil prices were high, and Mexico's oil industry made a great deal of money. Most of the oil at that time was found in Veracruz and Tabasco. In the 1980s, however, rich oil deposits were discovered beneath the floor of the Gulf of Mexico. Huge oil-drilling platforms now extract this valuable resource from the ocean floor.

Mineral mining

The first minerals to be mined in Mexico were gold and silver. Silver mining in particular brought much wealth to the Spanish colonial rulers. Mexico is still the world's largest producer of silver. The states of Guanajuato and San Luis Potosí in central Mexico are centers of silver-mining operations.

Iron and coal

Iron ore is mined in the northern state of Durango, and coal is mined in neighboring Coahuila. The city of Monterrey is an important center for iron and steel production. Many other minerals, including copper, tungsten, sulfur, lead, zinc, and uranium, are mined in Mexico.

Fishing

Most of the Mexican fishing industry is located along the coast of the Gulf of California. There, fishing crews haul in great quantities of sardines, red snapper, and shrimp. Most of the catch is exported to the United States. Beautiful silvery pearls are also gathered from oysters in the Gulf. The southern Pacific coasts are favorite spots for tourists, who fish for the marlin, swordfish, and sailfish that swim in the azure sea. The water off the Yucatán Peninsula teems with a variety of fish, including tuna, tarpon, red snapper, and mackerel. Fishing crews on the inland lakes use traditional fishing methods. Unfortunately, pollution in these lakes is threatening the fish and the livelihood of the people who depend on the catch.

(above) Fishing crews on Lake Pátzcuaro still use wide butterfly nets, named for their shape. This method has been used for generations.

Forestry

Although much of northern Mexico is too dry to support vast forests, there are wooded areas on the slopes of the Sierra Madres. Many of these pine and white cedar forests have been cut down to provide firewood and charcoal for neighboring towns and villages. Some of the lumber is used in the construction, furniture, and paper industries. The thick forests of southern Mexico, filled with mahogany, cedar, oak, and pine trees, have also been chopped down for lumber.

High-tech manufacturing

In the past few years, northern Mexico has become a growing center for high-tech manufacturing. Factories called *maquiladores* are owned and operated by foreign companies. Television sets, computers, and other items are produced in cities along the Mexico-United States border. Cars and trucks are assembled at plants located in northwest Mexico.

Visiting Mexico

Each winter, millions of tourists—mostly from the United States and Canada—visit Mexico. The tourism industry is extremely important to Mexico. It brings billions of dollars to the economy and employs millions of people.

Visitors enjoy shopping in Mexico City, sightseeing in colonial towns such as San Miguel de Allende, and exploring ancient Mayan ruins in the Yucatán. Swimming and scuba diving are popular pastimes at the beaches and resorts of Acapulco, Puerto Vallarta, Cancún, and Cozumel. Cultural attractions, tropical settings, and low prices make Mexico a favorite vacation spot for many travelers.

(top) The rainforests of southern Mexico are the source of many valuable varieties of wood.
(bottom) Parasailing is a popular sport among tourists. A speedboat pulls the parasailor high into the air.
(opposite page) Hotels employ millions of Mexicans.
(opposite page, inset) Silver jewelry is a great bargain for tourists. It is sold everywhere—even on the beach!

(above) Many farmers
still rely on outdated
equipment.
(middle) In Mexico,
riding horseback is
still the best way to
get around the farm.

(below) Mexico is the
world's sixth-largest
producer of meat. These
cattle are grazing in the
hills of Chiapas.

⚞ Agriculture ⚟

Agriculture has always been one of Mexico's most important industries. Before the Mexican Revolution in 1910, most farming was done on *haciendas*, or ranches. Some of these large farms were millions of acres in size. The wealthy owners employed peasants to work the land. They paid the peasants little and forced them to live in difficult conditions. This injustice was an important reason for the revolution.

Share the land

A new constitution was written in 1917. This document stated the laws that would govern Mexico. One law made the *haciendas* illegal and gave the government possession of the land. The land was distributed to the peasants, who were allowed to work the land as if it were their own. In 1991 the government finally permitted farmers to rent or buy their own land.

Irrigation

In many areas of Mexico, irrigation is essential to farming. Only one-fifth of the land is suitable for farming—the rest is either mountainous or dry and rocky. With the help of irrigation, cotton and wheat are now major crops in northern Mexico. In some coastal areas, scientists are experimenting with ways to take the salt out of ocean water in order to irrigate farmlands near the water.

Communal farms

Small farms are not as efficient as large farms. To be more efficient, small groups of farmers often band together to form large shared farms called *ejidos*. Unfortunately, many Mexican farmers lack agricultural training and modern equipment. Most of them still rely on horses to pull the same type of plow Mexicans have used for hundreds of years. Few farmers have enough money for new equipment. Despite these problems, one out of three Mexicans works in agriculture.

Corn, beans, and squash

Farmers raise sheep and cattle and grow crops of corn, tomatoes, coffee, and strawberries. The most important crops grown in Mexico are corn, beans, and squash. Corn, or *maíze*, is a major part of each Mexican's diet. It is usually ground and made into flat breads called *tortillas*. Beans, called *fríjoles*, are often cooked, then mashed and fried. Squash can be cooked many ways—boiled, baked, or fried. Mexicans do not eat much meat. These three vegetables provide the important vitamins and protein needed in their diet.

(above) Centuries-old farming techniques are still used by many Native farmers. As a result, their farms are not as profitable as more modern farms.

Transportation

The railroad

The railroad played an important part in developing the Mexican nation. Most of the railways were built between the years 1876 and 1910, during the dictatorship of Porfirio Díaz. He felt that the railroad would help in transporting resources and manufactured goods. Nearly 24,000 kilometers (15,000 miles) of track were laid. Building the railways was very difficult and costly. Bridges and tunnels had to be built over, through, and around the country's many mountains.

Today, most of Mexico's railways are owned and operated by the government. Many businesses consider the railroad slow and inefficient. They prefer to use trucks to transport their goods.

Roads and highways

Over the last 40 years the number of paved highways has increased greatly. There are now more than 70,000 kilometers (44,000 miles) of highway in Mexico. Remote parts of Mexico, such as Baja California and the Yucatán Peninsula, can now be reached by trucks and automobiles. Trucks are a very important means of transport for Mexican industries. Bus lines connecting major cities are a popular and easy way for Mexicans to take short trips to other parts of the country.

Ocean ports

Mexico's largest ports are at the cities of Tampico, Veracruz, Coatzacoalcos, Salina Cruz, Acapulco, Manzanillo, and Guaymas. Until recently, Mexico's ocean ports were owned and operated by the government. Many businesses found the ports old fashioned and costly to use. In the past few years, however, many ports have been sold to private companies. Private ownership has greatly improved the Mexican shipping industry.

Rural transportation

In some of the more remote parts of Mexico, people rely on forms of transportation that have been used for centuries. Burros, horses, and oxen are used to pull carts, carry riders, and drag plows. Most people in these undeveloped areas lack the money to buy tractors or automobiles.

Double trouble

If you were to journey across the Mexican countryside, you would see many bicycles carrying two riders. The passenger stands on two pegs, called *diablos,* which are attached to the rear axle of the bicycle. *Diablo* is the Spanish word for "devil." Can you think of a reason why these footholds have earned such a name?

(above) Burros are still a cheap, reliable form of transportation in Mexico.
(opposite page) No matter how you ride them, buses are a great way to get from place to place.
(opposite page, inset) The Métro, Mexico City's subway system, is one of the best subways in the world.

🐎 Mexico's cities 🐎

The cities of Mexico are a combination of traditional buildings and modern architecture. Though charming, these cities face many challenges. Each year thousands of Mexicans move there from the countryside to find jobs. The cities must provide housing, sanitation, and education for their new residents. Poverty, pollution, and overcrowding are growing problems in Mexico's big urban centers.

Massive Mexico City

With a population of more than 20 million people and growing, Mexico City is one of the largest cities in the world. One out of four Mexicans lives there! It is the capital of Mexico and the center of Mexico's industry, business, and culture. Mexico City was established in 1521 as the capital of the Spanish empire in North America. It was built over the site of the ancient Aztec capital of Tenochtitlán.

Guadalajara

The second-largest city in Mexico is Guadalajara. It is located near Lake Chapala and enjoys mild, sunny weather year round. Guadalajara has been very important to the development of western Mexico. Many beautiful churches and houses, as well as a university, were built there.

(above) The city of Guanajuato, a silver-mining center, is famous for its colonial architecture.
(opposite page, top) The Metropolitan Cathedral in Mexico City sits on the edge of a square called the Zócalo.
(opposite page, circle) Constant traffic jams are a way of life in Mexican cities.

Guadalajara is a city that loves soccer—it is home to four professional teams! It is also a center for the manufacturing of ceramics and a strong alcoholic drink called *tequila.*

Monterrey
This large northern city, the third largest in Mexico, is a center of business. Many corporations and industries are located there, including huge steel mills. Monterrey is also home to three large universities. The most famous is the Monterrey Institute of Technology and Higher Education, which trains Mexican students in the sciences.

Air pollution
The millions of people who live in Mexico's cities are the owners of millions of cars. Terrible traffic jams occur every day. The exhaust from the cars and buses, along with pollution from factories, has contributed to a thick layer of smog that hovers over each city.

Laws limiting emissions from cars and factories have not been very effective. In the future, new programs for public transportation and stronger pollution controls may help ease the smog. If these efforts do not work, the cities of Mexico could face even worse environmental problems.

🐊 Wildlife and the environment 🐊

Many parts of Mexico, such as Baja California, the northern deserts, and southern Mexico, are inhabited by few people. These regions are still refuges for millions of species of plants and animals.

Refuge in the desert

Several animals that are endangered in the southwestern United States are still plentiful in Baja California. The desert tortoise and the poisonous Gila monster are among the reptiles that live in this harsh area. The remote hills of the peninsula are a refuge for the desert big-horn sheep and hunting grounds for the puma.

A bevy of butterflies

Each winter, the eastern part of Michoacán state is swarmed by millions of visitors from the north. They are not tourists—they are monarch butterflies! Scientists are not sure why these large, orange-and-black insects travel hundreds of miles each year to this spot. Unfortunately, the butterflies may be in danger because logging operations are destroying their forest habitat.

The jungles of the south

The lush forests of southern Mexico, the Gulf of Mexico coast, and the Yucatán Peninsula are home to many varieties of animals. The black howler monkey and the spider monkey live in

the jungles, as do tapirs and peccaries. Several species of cats, including the jaguar, margay, and ocelot, hunt in the wilderness areas. Flocks of brilliant pink flamingos fly over the swamps of the Yucatán.

The famous gray whale

The most famous animal in Baja California lives in the area's turquoise coastal waters. In the nineteenth century, whalers hunted the gray whale for its blubber. By 1937 there were only 250 still living. Today these animals are protected, and nearly 20,000 gray whales live in the Gulf of Mexico. The gray whale spends its winters there after migrating from its summer home in the Arctic Ocean. Each year, tourists travel to the Gulf in hope of catching a glimpse of this majestic animal.

(above) The colors of the helmeted basilisk help it blend in with the leaves and branches of Mexico's forests.
(opposite page, top) The coatamundi loves climbing trees to find fruit, eggs, and insects to eat.
(opposite page, middle left) Eleutherodactylus frogs are different from most frogs. They are born as small frogs, not tadpoles.
(opposite page, bottom right) When it is older, this margay kitten will hunt for birds, frogs, and rodents.
(opposite page, bottom left) It may look ferocious, but this kind of bat eats only fruit.

Disappearing forests

Over the past several years, the forests of Mexico have been cut down at a rapid rate. Logging operations are part of the problem. Although logging has brought economic reward to some people, it has also meant the destruction of unique and beautiful wilderness areas. Farming is also to blame. Peasants have burned or chopped down forests to create more farmland. As a result, many plants and animals are endangered because they have lost their natural habitat.

La Ruta Maya

La Ruta Maya means "The Mayan Route." It is the name of an ambitious project planned by the governments of Mexico, Belize, Guatemala, El Salvador, and Honduras. The Route will be a road connecting several large protected wildlife areas in Mexico and Central America. In Mexico, the largest areas will be the Calakmul, Montes Azules, and Sian Ka'an biosphere reserves. The reserves feature lush rainforest and long-hidden Mayan cities. They are home to many endangered animal species. The Mayan Route will open these remote areas to visitors and allow local villages to benefit from tourist dollars. Some people worry that the powerful logging companies will oppose the protection of this land and stop the project.

(circle) The black howler monkey was worshipped as a god by the Maya.
(bottom) The Baird's tapir is very rare because much of its rainforest habitat has been destroyed.

Glossary

ally A partner during war or a time of conflict

archaeologist A person who studies the past through buildings and artifacts

archduke A nobleman of high rank

architecture The design and structure of buildings

azure A clear, light shade of blue

barren Unable to produce or support life

Bering Strait A channel of water that separates northeast Asia from northwest North America

bevy A flock of flying animals

biosphere An ecosystem; an area in which plant and animal life sustain each other

burro A small donkey

ceramic Delicate pottery made from a white clay

coatamundi A raccoon-like animal found from southern United States to South America

colonial Describing or relating to a land or people ruled by a distant country

congress A government body that makes decisions and passes laws

deciduous Describing trees, such as the maple or oak, that lose their leaves in the winter

dictator A ruler who has complete power

dune A mound of shifting sand on a beach or desert

empire A group of countries under one ruler

engineer A person who designs buildings and other structures

ethnic Describing or relating to social groups connected by race, language, heritage, or religion

extinct Not in existence; no longer living in the wild

federation A group of states or regions that unite under one government

habitat The natural environment of a plant or animal

humid Moist; damp

irrigate To water crops using artificial channels or streams that run through fields

land baron A person who owns huge amounts of property

limestone Calcium-filled rock that is formed from decayed plants

margay A breed of small, spotted wild cat that lives in Central and South America

marlin A species of large, long-nosed fish

metropolis A large city

migrate To move from one place to another

monument A structure dedicated to a person or event

New World The name given to North, South, and Central America by sixteenth-century explorers

ocelot A breed of cat similar to the margay, but with a shorter tail and a narrower face

ore A naturally occurring mineral from which a metal is extracted

peasant A farmer who works land belonging to others

peccary A wild pig that lives in Central and South America

peninsula A point of land that juts into a body of water

plateau A flat, high-altitude landform

protein Chemicals that are necessary for growth and health, found in foods such as eggs, meat, and milk

rainforest A dense forest that receives a great deal of rainfall

refine To purify

refuge A place safe from danger

revenue Income; money earned

revolution A war in which the people of a country fight against the government

Roman Catholic church An organization of Christians headed by the pope

smog A mixture of smoke and fog

sulfur A yellow rock found near volcanoes and hot springs, used in making gunpowder and various chemicals

tapir A horselike tropical animal that sleeps during the day and is active at night

tarpon A large saltwater fish

tungsten A rare metal used in producing, among other things, electric light bulbs

turbine An engine powered by a wheel that is turned by water, steam, or air

uranium A mineral used in creating nuclear energy

zinc A hard, bluish-white mineral that is used in making brass

✦ Index ✦

agriculture 8, 22-23, 30
Angel of Independence 9
architecture 6, 7, 15, 27
Aztecs 4, 7, 10, 16, 17, 26
Baja California 10, 25, 28
Cascada Agua Azul 12
Central America 6, 30
Central Highlands 10
Central Plateau 10, 11
cities 26-27
Citlaltépetl 10, 16
Copper Canyon 11
Cortés, Hernán 4, 7, 9
criollos 9
deserts 10, 11, 28
Díaz, Porfirio 8, 25
earthquakes 14-15
ejidos 23
factories 18, 20, 27
fishing 19
gray whale 28
Guadalajara 26, 27
Guanajuato 27
Gulf Lowlands 12
Gulf of California 10, 19, 28
Gulf of Mexico 10, 12, 19, 28
haciendas 23
Hidalgo, Father 8
highways 25
history of Mexico 6-9
hydroelectricity 18
Institutional Revolutionary Party 9
irrigation 23
Iztaccíhuatl 17
Lake Chapala 10, 26
Lake Pátzcuaro 10, 19
La Ruta Maya 30
Latin American Tower 15
logging 12, 20, 28, 30
Maximilian, Emperor 8
Maya 6, 7, 20, 30
mestizos 8, 9
Mexico City 7, 9, 14, 15, 16, 20, 25, 26, 27

minerals 8, 19, 27
monarch butterflies 28
Monterrey 19, 27
Montezuma II 7
mulattos 9
Native civilizations 4, 6, 7
Native peoples 6, 7, 8, 9, 18, 23
natural resources 8, 18-20
Neo-volcanic Cordillera 10
Northwest Region 10
ocean ports 25
oil 19
Olmecs 6
Orizaba see Citlaltépetl
overpopulation 9, 18, 26
Palenque 7
Paricutín 16
Pemex (Petróleos Mexicanos) 19
plate tectonics 14, 16
pollution 19, 26, 27
Popocatépetl 16, 17
Quetzalcoatl 7
railroad 25
rainforest 12, 20, 30
regions 10-13
revolution of 1810 8
revolution of 1910 8, 23
San Lorenzo 6
San Miguel de Allende 20
Sierra Madres 10, 12, 20
sinkholes 12
Southern Region 12
Spanish 4, 7, 8, 9, 19, 26
Tenochtitlán 7, 26
Teotihuacán 6
tourism 12, 18, 19, 20, 28, 30
transportation 24-25
unemployment 18
United States 8, 19, 20, 28
volcanoes 10, 16-17
wildlife 28-30
Yucatán Peninsula 6, 12, 19, 20, 25, 28
Zapotecs 6

1 2 3 4 5 6 7 8 9 0   Printed in the U.S.A.   2 1 0 9 8 7 6 5 4 3